THE

BENCH

THAT

WAITED

PATRICIA S. TANNER

IBG Publications, Inc.

PATRICIA S. TANNER

IBG
PUBLICATIONS
Putting the POWER in your pen!

Published by I.B.G. Publications, LLC, a Power to Wealth Company

Web address: www.ibgpublications.com

admin@ibgpublications.com / 904-419-9810

Copyright, 2025 by Patricia S. Tanner

IBG Publications, Inc., Orange Park, FL

ISBN: 978-1-956266-86-3

Tanner, Patricia S.
The Bench That Waited

Printed in the United States of America.

DEDICATION

To every soul who sat, stayed, and silently wondered if there was more—this is for you.

To the weary churchgoer whose heart outgrew the pew, To the quiet worshipper who clapped on cue but cried in silence, To the one who dared to get up while others stayed seated—You are the reason this book was written.

And to the Holy Spirit the true Author of awakening, who refused to let me get comfortable on the bench, thank You for whispering, convicting, and calling me to rise.

May this book stir the stagnant, shake the slumbering, and send the seated.

The bench has waited long enough.

Now it's time to move.

—Patricia S. Tanner

PATRICIA S. TANNER

TABLE OF CONTENTS

INTRODUCTION

A Silent Witness.

Let's just get this out of the way—I didn't plan to write yet another book about church folks. Honestly, I've sat on the same benches, watched the same routines, and nodded through sermons that stirred zero transformation. I've clapped on cue, dropped my tithe in the bucket, and smiled at people I didn't really want to speak to.

Been there. Done that. Nearly printed the T-shirt.

But something kept gnawing at me. Not a voice from the clouds, not a lightning bolt from the heavens—just a deep ache. A restlessness. A silent shout coming from somewhere in the back row of the sanctuary. And that's when it hit me: we're showing up, but we're not standing up. We're in the building, but we're not being built.

I wasn't lying awake at night dreaming of becoming the next spiritual self-help guru, and I certainly wasn't hoping to add more noise to the already-overcrowded Christian bookshelf section at your local store. In fact, I tried not to write this. I shrugged it off. Told God, "There are already too many books for people who are already going to church."

But that's exactly the problem, isn't it? People 'are going' to church. They're just not ***going*** anywhere else. They're not going deeper. They're not changing. They're not applying. They're just… going.

This book was born from that discomfort—from the sense that we've mastered church attendance but forgotten Kingdom advancement. It's for the ones who've grown numb in the pew, bored with the performance, frustrated with the pretense, and quietly desperate for something real.

So no, this isn't another sugarcoated devotional guide. This is a spiritual wake-up call for those still warming benches while their purpose is collecting dust. It's not polite. It's not polished. But it's packed with the truth you've been dodging, and the freedom you didn't know you were missing.

The Waiting Bench

There it sat, year after year. The same bench. The same seat. The same spot on the third row, near the aisle. It held hundreds of bodies, thousands of conversations, and more Sunday suits than any department store ever sold. It had become a place of habit, a spiritual landing strip for routines, traditions, and appearances. For all the people who had ever sat on one yet had never really moved.

If the bench could speak, what would it say? Would it whisper about the Sunday morning saints who shouted "Hallelujah" but walked out bitter? Would it recount the tears shed during worship that were never turned into change? Would it remember the gossip it overheard after service, or the weight of hands that clapped during praise but never lifted to help the hurting? Would it sigh under the weight of bodies that grew heavier with knowledge, but never lighter from obedience?

This is not a book about furniture. It's about the lives that sat still while pretending to move. It's about the pews that are full, but hearts that are empty. It's about the people who go to church every week, not to meet God, but to meet expectations. Not to be changed, but to be seen. Not to grow, but to blend in. They've been attending service for years, yet their spiritual posture is the same. Still sitting. Still watching. Still waiting.

And the bench—well, it waited too.

The Times We Live In

We live in an era where church has become more of a routine than a revival. People dress up their bodies but leave their spirits naked. They raise their hands out of rhythm, not reverence. They show up because it's what they've always done.

Church has become a spiritual social club for some—where the point is to be seen, not to be transformed. We've traded authentic encounters with God for emotional entertainment. We shout during the sermon but stay silent when truth demands a response. We are more familiar with religious performance than we are with genuine repentance.

This book is for every person who has ever felt that church was something they attended, not someone they became. It's for those who grew up in pews, who know all the songs, all the scriptures, all the motions—but deep inside, they know they've never truly stood up. It's for those who feel numb to sermons, who feel disconnected in worship, who feel like they're just going through the motions and wondering if God still speaks, if God still moves, if church still matters.

Facing The Truth

Let's be honest: we've mastered the look of holiness while quietly drowning in spiritual apathy. We clap on beat, quote the pastor, shout on cue—but walk out with no change in how we live, love, give, or grow.

We've sat so long that the bench has memorized our shape. It knows where our shoulders slump in defeat. It knows what we lean on when we're distracted. It knows how to hold us in comfort when conviction knocks at our door, and we refuse to answer.

And while we sit, the bench waits. It waits for movement. It waits for repentance. It waits for a breakthrough. It waits for us to realize that God didn't save us to sit, He saved us to stand—to move, to live, to transform.The modern church is in crisis, not because there aren't enough seats, but because there aren't enough souls standing up.

We've made sitting a symbol of safety. We sit on promises we never act on. We sat on words that were meant to stir us to action. We sat on gifts that were meant to be poured out. And yet we wonder why nothing is changing. We keep waiting for revival, while revival waits on us.

In **James 1:22**, the scripture rings clear and convicting: *"Do not merely listen to the word and so deceive yourselves. **Do** what it says."*

The danger is not in the hearing—but in the deception that hearing is enough. It's not. The Word of God is not a lecture—it's a lifeline. It's not a suggestion—it's a summons. It was never meant to entertain us; it was meant to equip us.

You see, every bench in every church has a story. Some hold the weight of quiet desperation, people too afraid to speak out, too tired to pray. Others carry the weight of arrogance, convinced they already know enough, already do enough. And then there are those benches that ache with potential, longing to see the person sitting on them finally rise into their calling. To finally take seriously what they've been hearing for years. To finally stop waiting for someone else to do it. To finally become more than a consumer of the gospel—to become a doer.

This book, The Bench That Waited, is not just a critique. It's a cry. A call. A wake-up siren to those who are sleeping in the sanctuary. It's a mirror for the churchgoer who knows deep down that sitting is no longer enough. It's a challenge to those who've gotten comfortable on the bench, to remember the fire that once burned in them—or maybe, to discover it for the first time.

We will walk through the distractions, the pretenses, the gossip, the routine. We will sit on the bench together and ask hard questions:

- ✓ *Why am I here?*
- ✓ *What have I done with what I've heard?*
- ✓ *When did church become a habit and not a home?*

And then, by God's grace, we'll stand. We'll rise from routine. We'll move toward purpose. Because the gospel demands more than sitting through service. It demands transformation.

There is a world beyond the bench. A purpose beyond the pew. A calling beyond comfort. But first, we must acknowledge the seat we've claimed and the life we've refused to live while sitting in it. This is your moment to stand. This is the book the bench has been waiting for.

And somewhere between the pews and the pulpit, something holy got traded for something hollow. We clapped for sermons we never lived out. We said "amen" to words that never hit home. We got really, really good at showing up and sitting down—but almost allergic to standing in truth, walking in purpose, or serving with sincerity.

I started noticing the little things:

- The same faces in the same seats, week after week, like assigned spiritual parking spots.
- The nods of agreement that never led to any real action.
- The prayer requests for breakthrough from people who refused to break free from bad habits.
- The gospel we claimed to love… somehow collecting dust in our Monday-through- Saturday lives

And it wasn't just one church. It wasn't just one city. It was everywhere. So, after years of watching the benches bear the weight of bodies that wouldn't budge, I realized—maybe it's not the sermons that are broken. Maybe it's our posture. Maybe we've confused participation with transformation. Maybe we've mistaken being present for being purposeful.

Who Is This Book For?

This book is for those of you who've felt the disconnect but couldn't quite name it. You know something's off. You've felt the tug. You've left church wondering, "Is this it? Is this all I'm supposed to do?" You're not alone. You're not crazy. And no, this book isn't coming for your salvation—it's coming for your stagnation.

It's a conversation with every person who ever dressed up in their Sunday best, shouted through the message, posted a selfie outside the sanctuary—and then quietly went home to a life that looked nothing like Jesus. It's for the exhausted, the distracted, the numb, the habitual, and the well-meaning Christians who haven't stood up in their faith in a long, long time.

This isn't about judgment—it's about awakening.

The benches have waited long enough. They've held you through your good intentions, your spiritual apathy, your quiet disobedience. But the call of God is not to sit until you feel something. It's to move even when you don't. To respond even when it's uncomfortable. To live like you believe what you *say* you believe.

So yeah… it's another church book. But this one is different. Because it's not for the ones who are content sitting down. It's for the ones who are ready to finally stand up.

CHAPTER 1

THE BENCH THAT WAITED

• The Symbol of the Bench–A metaphor for spiritual stillness and unfulfilled purpose.

• A Seat of Comfort, Not Conviction–How church benches become enablers of spiritual complacency.

• Attendance vs. Activation–The difference between going to church and growing in God.

• When Sitting Becomes a Spiritual Posture–How we normalize in action.

• The Cry of the Pew–What the church building would say if it could speak.

"Arise, shine, for your light has come, and the glory of the Lord rises upon you."
—**Isaiah 60:1 (NIV)**

The Symbol of the Bench

The bench is more than furniture; it's a symbol of spiritual stagnation. In churches across the world, benches have become silent witnesses to the rise and fall of faith journeys. They represent the habit of showing up without engaging, of presence without purpose. The bench doesn't demand anything from us—it simply waits. It welcomes whoever sits on it, whether on fire for God or numb to His presence. But that passivity reflects what many Christians have become: settled, still, and spiritually asleep.

A Seat of Comfort, Not Conviction

Church has become a place of comfort for many, and the bench plays a part. It's where we go to rest from the world, but too often it becomes where we hide from change. The comfort of routine and predictability dulls our sensitivity to God's voice. We begin to believe that if we're in the building, we must be in the will. But the truth is, the bench has held too many of us hostage, letting us sit through conviction instead of responding to it.

Attendance vs. Activation

We are not called to be spiritual spectators. Attendance in church is not the finish line; it's the starting gate. God is not measuring how many Sundays we sat through, but how we applied what we heard. Activation means stepping off the bench and into our God- given assignment. But too often, people believe that just being present is enough. This lie has kept believers from fulfilling purpose, volunteering, sharing the gospel, and walking in spiritual authority.

The Bench and the Mask —
A Comfortable Place to Hide.

The Show We All Know

Every Sunday morning, church pews fill with bodies and smiles. The sanctuary becomes a stage where we rehearse the same spiritual lines: "God is good," "I'm blessed and highly favored," or "Everything is fine." But behind the smiles lies a silent epidemic— people show up in the building but hiding in plain sight. We dress the part. We know the motions. We clap at the right moment. Yet, our hearts remain untouched. It's easier to play the role than to be real. The bench, then, becomes a safe place to blend in, to avoid confrontation, to dodge the Word that calls us out.

Beneath the fabric of Sunday fashion, people carry burdens that never make it to the altar. Mental anguish, marital despair, identity struggles, addictions masked as victories, all tucked neatly beneath praise hands and polite nods. The mask is easier than the mirror. Looking deeply would require change, and for many, the bench provides a convenient excuse to postpone transformation. It's where people come to watch but never witness, to sit but never surrender.

Routine Over Revelation

The tragedy of the modern church is not that people have stopped coming—but that they've stopped encountering. We've reduced worship to routine and made the altar an accessory. For many, church is no longer a spiritual encounter but a social expectation. It's the thing to do before brunch. It's where your parents went. It's where you feel safe, not stretched. The message goes forth with power, but it falls on distracted ears. The anointing flows, but many are checking the clock.

Spiritual growth requires hunger. Revelation requires intention. But routine dulls hunger and numbs intention. You can't receive a prophetic word with a passive heart. You can't grow in the Kingdom while coasting through service after service with no intention to change. When the routine replaces reverence, we trade power for performance. The church bench becomes not just a place to sit, but a place to spiritually sleep.

The Psychology Of Passive Faith

Why do we hide? Why do we settle for shallow faith? Psychology offers some insight.

People crave certainty and comfort. In a world full of anxiety, fear, and instability, the bench offers predictability. No one calls you out. No one expects much from you. You're invisible in a crowd of the "faithful." But the price of comfort is calling. When we silence conviction long enough, we begin to believe that faith is just about showing up, not showing fruit.

Cognitive dissonance also plays a role. We want to see ourselves as "good Christians," yet we ignore the commands of Christ. To resolve the inner conflict, we rationalize our passivity. "At least I go to church," we say. "I'm better than most." But God doesn't grade on a curve—He calls for our whole heart. The longer we sit, the harder it is to move. Paralysis becomes normal, and the bench becomes home.

The Bench Becomes a Battlefield

The spiritual war isn't always in the world—it's on the bench. Every Sunday, sermons go forth that could break chains, restore minds, and awaken destinies—but many never hear them beyond the surface. The enemy whispers lies to benchwarmers: "You're too broken to serve." "You don't belong here." "Just keep your head down and your heart closed."

But there's a war behind those whispers. The enemy isn't afraid of you attending church, he's afraid of you *becoming* the church. He'll let you show up as long as you stay silent, stagnant, and spiritually sleepy. But the moment you realize the bench isn't your destiny, heaven starts clapping and hell starts trembling.

From Attender To Altar Builder

The bench was never meant to be your final stop. It's a place to rest, not a place to rot. God is calling for altar builders—people who turn their sitting into surrender, who trade their seat for service, who stop spectating and start sanctifying. The altar is waiting. God's voice is calling. And your life is meant for more than passive proximity.

You were never created to hide behind a mask or find comfort in complacency. You were created to carry the glory of God into every corner of your life. The bench may have waited, but the time has come to rise!

When Sitting Becomes a Spiritual Posture

There's a difference between sitting physically and spiritually. Some people sit down in their hearts long before they ever stop serving. They sit on their convictions, sit on their callings, and sit on their burdens. They're still showing up, but they aren't showing out in faith. The bench is not just a seat—it becomes a mindset. It trains us to settle, to defer, to postpone obedience. Eventually, we normalize being unbothered by spiritual laziness.

The Cry of the Pew

If the pew could talk, it would beg us to move. It would ask, "Why do you keep hearing the truth but refusing to live it?" It would question how long we plan to sit on gifts, dreams, and convictions. The pew holds stories of breakthrough delayed and lives never lived to their full potential. It groans under the weight of believers with unrealized callings.

THE BENCH THAT WAITED

It's time to listen to the cry of the pew and get up!

"SPIRITUAL BENCHES DON'T JUST HOLD BODIES—THEY HOLD DELAYED DESTINIES. BUT THE MOMENT YOU RISE, THE WAIT ENDS."

—Patricia S. Tanner

CHAPTER 2

DRESSED BUT SPIRITUALLY UNDONE

• Faith as Fashion–When church becomes a runway, not a sanctuary.

• Outward Holiness, Inward Emptiness–Wearing religion but lacking relationship.

• The Pressure to Appear "Blessed"–Image vs. reality in today's Christian circles.

• Comparison in the Congregation–When focus shifts from worship to wardrobe.

• Jesus, Not Just Jewelry–Moving beyond accessorizing God to embodying Him.

"Woe to you, teachers of the law and Pharisees, you hypocrites! You are like whitewashed tombs, which look beautiful on the outside but on the inside are full of the bones of the dead and everything unclean."
—**Matthew 23:27 (NIV)**

Faith as Fashion

We live in an era where faith is often more about appearance than authenticity. Sunday best has become a brand. Instagram-worthy outfits, polished personas, and curated public images now overshadow real spiritual depth. Dressing up is fine, but it must not be a substitute for dressing inwardly in righteousness. Faith isn't a costume to put on once a week.

Outward Holiness, Inward Emptiness

Jesus rebuked the Pharisees for looking clean on the outside but being full of dead men's bones on the inside. That same spirit is alive today. Many Christians have learned how to "play church" while their inner lives are in chaos. We can quote scripture but can't apply it. We lead ministries but are emotionally unstable. This double life is not sustainable and leads to burnout, depression, and spiritual deception.

The Pressure To Appear "Blessed"

Social media has exacerbated the pressure to appear perfect. Testimonies have been replaced with "aesthetic" posts. Instead of sharing real struggles and victories, we curate highlight reels of blessings. This creates a toxic cycle of comparison, causing others to feel like failures when they don't see instant breakthroughs. God isn't looking for filtered faith; He's looking for surrendered hearts.

Comparison in the Congregation

One of the most dangerous cancers in the church is comparison. Instead of being inspired by others' growth, we resent it. We dress to impress rather than express gratitude. We judge others based on surface-level behavior while ignoring our own internal battles. This not only damages the community, but it also hinders personal growth. When we're busy looking side to side, we can't focus on the upward call of God.

Jesus, Not Just Jewelry

Wearing a cross around your neck doesn't mean you carry one in your life. Jesus is not an accessory. He's not something we match with our outfits or pull out when we need a miracle. He is a Savior, Lord, and King. When we reduce Him to a Sunday symbol, we strip Him of His power in our daily lives. We need to move from fashion to faithfulness.

Worship Without Transformation — The Sound Of Empty Praise

The Noise Of Religion

Worship has become a performance in many churches—lights, haze, perfectly rehearsed teams, tight transitions. The music is flawless, the vocals stunning. But God doesn't respond to performance—He responds to purity. You can raise your hands and still not raise your heart. You can weep during worship and walk out unchanged.

Isaiah 29:13 says, *"These people come near to me with their mouth and honor me with their lips, but their hearts are far from me."*

Sound familiar?

We've perfected the language of praise but neglected the posture of transformation. True worship demands a yielded life, not just a lifted voice.

Emotional Highs, Spiritual Lows

Many mistake emotional experiences for spiritual growth. We chase the *"feeling"* of God, not the formation of God. We want goosebumps but not growth. We want inspiration but not instruction. The moment the music fades, so does our commitment. Real transformation requires more than moments—it requires movement.

Worship should lead to repentance. It should break chains, not just break a sweat. But when worship becomes entertainment, it loses its eternal power. We must stop settling for good music and start hungering for God's presence. True worship alters our appetites. It makes us holy. It brings Heaven down and lifts us up.

The Heart That God Hears

THE BENCH THAT WAITED

Psalm 51:17 says, *"The sacrifices of God are a broken spirit; a broken and contrite heart, O God, you will not despise."*

God listens to hearts, not harmonies. A heart in surrender sounds louder in heaven than a full band on stage. You don't need a perfect pitch, you need purity. You don't need drums, you need devotion.

When the heart bows, the heavens open. Worship is less about songs and more about submission. It's when you say, "God, take all of me," even if all you have is broken. It's when your life begins to sing louder than your lips. That's when transformation begins.

From Hype To Holiness

We've created a culture of hype, but God is calling us back to holiness. Hype fades. Holiness lingers. Hype impresses. Holiness transforms. Holiness means living a life set apart—where worship spills into Monday, not just Sunday. It's how you treat others, how you make decisions, how you fight temptation, and how you reflect Christ daily.

Holiness is not perfection—it's direction. It's a heart bent toward God. And worship is the furnace where holiness is formed. If our worship doesn't drive us to love more deeply, forgive more freely, and serve more sacrificially, then we're just making noise.

Worship That Walks

The highest praise is not in a song—it's in a life that obeys. Worship that doesn't change you isn't worship at all. It's a show. But when your praise walks with you into hard places—into the office, into the conflict, into the dark nights—then your life becomes the altar, and your obedience becomes the fragrance.

Romans 12:1 calls us to *"present your bodies as a living sacrifice, holy and acceptable to God, which is your spiritual worship."*

Worship that walks is worship that works. It labors in love. It forgives when it hurts. It shows up with joy when sorrow seems louder. That's the sound God listens for—not just what we sing, but what we live.

"GOD IS NOT IMPRESSED WITH YOUR OUTFIT IF YOUR SOUL IS STILL NAKED. HEAVEN SEES THROUGH WHAT SUNDAY COVERS UP."

— Patricia S. Tanner

CHAPTER 3

WORSHIP WITHOUT WEIGHT

• Performing Praise—Singing and shouting but never surrendering.

• Heartless Hallelujahs—Worship disconnected from personal transformation.

• The Emotional High Trap—Confusing goosebumps with growth.

• Distracted in God's Presence—Phones in hand, minds elsewhere.

• Spirit and Truth Revisited—What God truly desires from worship.

"These people honor me with their lips, but their hearts are far from me. They worship me in vain; their teachings are merely human rules."
—**Matthew 15:8–9 (NIV)**

Performing Praise

Many churches have turned worship into a performance. Lights, fog machines, and rehearsed songs are fine until they replace authentic reverence. God is not moved by perfect pitch; He's moved by broken hearts. True worship isn't about volume or style—it's about spirit and truth. When we praise without heart, we entertain men but not God.

Heartless Hallelujahs

How many times have we lifted our hands out of habit? Said "amen" just to fit in? When worship becomes routine, it loses its weight. The danger lies in singing songs that no longer move us. Worship is meant to be costly, to stretch us, to confront us. When it becomes background noise, we miss the divine encounter it was meant to produce.

The Emotional High Trap

Worship should stir emotion, but emotion is not the goal. Too many believers equate emotional experiences with spiritual growth. You can cry every Sunday and still walk out unchanged. The danger of emotionalism is that it mimics transformation without requiring commitment. We need worship that leads to renewed minds, not just wet eyes.

Distracted in God's Presence

Phones buzzing, minds drifting, people scrolling; distractions are robbing us of intimacy. Even in the sanctuary, many are more connected to their notifications than their Creator. Reverence for God's presence is being lost. We must reclaim focus and discipline in worship, treating every moment in His presence as sacred and supernatural.

Spirit and Truth Revisited

Jesus told the woman at the well that the Father seeks those who worship in spirit and truth. Not talent and technique. Not appearance and aesthetics. Spirit and truth require honesty, vulnerability, and a heart that thirsts for God. This is where real transformation begins— not on stage, but in surrendered hearts.

The Spiritually Sleepwalking Saints — When Believers Stop Feeling

Walking, But Not Awake

There is a haunting phenomenon quietly sweeping through the pews, pulpits, and prayer meetings of today's church—a deep spiritual slumber. People are moving, singing, working in ministry, attending conferences, and showing up on Sundays, yet inwardly they are asleep. Their hands may be raised, but their hearts are numb. Their feet may be moving, but their spirits are stuck. These are the 'spiritually sleepwalking' saints—alive but not alert, present but not passionate.

We often picture spiritual warfare as dramatic confrontations, loud prayers, and casting out demons. But one of the enemy's most subtle tactics is sedation. He lulls believers into routine. He rocks them into ritual. He whispers lies that life is "fine as it is," as long as they stay distracted and detached.

Many live in a half-awake haze—minds preoccupied with the day-to-day, hearts dulled by disappointment, and souls robbed of purpose. It's not that they've stopped believing. It's that they've stopped burning.

The Symptoms Of Spiritual Slumber

Spiritual slumber doesn't look like rebellion. It often wears the mask of "normal." You still attend service, still read a devotional now and then, still say grace over meals. But inwardly, the flame is gone.

Symptoms include:

- A loss of hunger for God's Word.

- Apathy toward sin.

- Cynicism toward the supernatural.

- Numbness in prayer.

- Increased tolerance for distractions.

You begin to drift. You say things like, "I'm just tired," or "I'm just busy," not realizing that spiritual dehydration is setting in. Church becomes a chore. Scripture feels dull. Worship feels like background noise. And slowly, your passion is replaced with passivity.

You're not lost— you're lulled.

THE BENCH THAT WAITED

What Causes the Slumber?

The reasons vary. For some, it's disappointment. Prayers that went unanswered. Loss that was never processed. Trauma covered in church language but never truly healed. For others, it's burnout—serving, giving, leading without rest or real connection. Ministry became maintenance, and they confused movement with intimacy.

Still, for many others, it's distraction. The slow creep of compromise. The constant ping of a phone. The false comfort of entertainment. The hustle of ambition. A little less time in prayer. A little more time scrolling. And before you know it, your soul has drifted ten miles from where it once stood.

God's Alarm Clock

But God, in His mercy, sounds the alarm. He stirs the spirit. He allows discomfort. He interrupts your peace. Sometimes, He lets a relationship fall apart. Sometimes, He lets you get to the end of your own strength. Sometimes, He simply asks, "Where are you?" like He did with Adam. Not because He doesn't know—but because you forgot.

Romans 13:11 says, *"The hour has already come for you to wake up from your slumber, because our salvation is nearer now than when we first believed."* God's alarm doesn't come to shame—it comes to shake. Shake you free from autopilot. Shake you back into purpose. Shake you into remembering who you are and why you were called.

The Awakening Begins Within

Spiritual awakening doesn't always begin in a revival tent. Often, it begins in the silence of your bedroom. When you whisper, *"God,*

I'm dry." When you admit, "I've been going through the motions." When you fall to your knees not out of obligation but desperation. Awakening begins when honesty returns. When hunger is resurrected.

Don't wait for someone to lay hands on you. Lay your life on the altar. Return to your first love. Go back to the place where His voice was loudest. Tear down the distractions. Starve the apathy. Reignite the flame.

You Were Made To Burn

Hebrews 12:29 says, *"Our God is a consuming fire."* If you belong to Him, then that same fire should live in you. Not just a flicker, but a force. You were never meant to settle for lukewarm. Jesus said He would rather we be cold or hot—but lukewarm makes Him nauseous (**Revelation 3:15-16**). And yet, how many saints have chosen to live in the gray?

You were made to burn. To burn with compassion. To burn with truth. To burn with holiness. Not a fire of hype, but of holy pursuit. Not loud, fake spiritual noise—but deep, consistent communion. That's what the world is waiting for. Not just churchgoers—but fire carriers.

So, wake up, saint. Shake yourself. Get back in the Word. Turn your heart toward Heaven. Let the bench witness your rise. The world needs your fire. And God is ready to breathe on your soul once more.

CHAPTER 4

THE CHURCH HABIT

- Going Without Growing–How routine attendance numbs spiritual hunger.

- Tradition Over Transformation–When habit replaces hunger.

- Inherited Faith, Forgotten Fire–Generational attendance without personal conviction.

- Church as Calendar, Not Calling–Sunday religion vs. weekday relationship.

- Routine That Replaces Reverence– The danger of spiritual autopilot.

"'These people come near to me with their mouth and honor me with their lips, but their hearts are far from me. Their worship of me is based merely on human rules they have been taught.'"
—**Isaiah 29:13 (NIV)**

Going Without Growing

It's possible to attend church for years and never grow spiritually. Attendance does not equal discipleship. Many have confused being around the things of God with becoming like Him. Just because you sit in a garage doesn't make you a car; likewise, sitting in church doesn't make you Christlike. Growth requires intention, not proximity.

Tradition Over Transformation

Some believers are more loyal to their traditions than to the truth. They defend church customs that no longer bear fruit. Traditions are valuable when they lead to life, but when they replace the living Word, they become idols. God is not impressed by how long you've kept a routine—He's looking for fruit.

Inherited Faith, Forgotten Fire

Generational Christianity can become cultural Christianity if the fire isn't passed down. Too many have inherited beliefs but never had a personal encounter with Jesus. They attend church because their parents did but have no relationship with God.

Faith cannot be inherited, it must be encountered, ignited, and owned.

Church As Calendar, Not Calling

Church has become a line item on a weekly schedule, like a grocery run or a gym visit. But God never called us to schedule Him in. He called us to surrender our entire lives. Church is not an appointment; it's the launching point for Kingdom living. Our calling is to carry the presence of God everywhere we go, not just within four walls.

Routine That Replaces Reverence

When we treat holy things as common, we lose their power. Routine can dull our sense of awe. We stop expecting miracles, stop listening for God's voice, stop approaching His presence with fear and trembling. The fire fades when reverence is replaced with religious repetition. We must return to the wonder of who God is.

When The Curtain Falls

For many, faith begins in the warm embrace of community—church services, youth groups, worship nights filled with hope and hallelujahs. But eventually, life demands something deeper than what was inherited. When the emotional high wears off, when the prayer circle disbands, when the crisis doesn't end in a miracle— what remains? The harsh slopes of reality. That's when people discover whether they've been climbing with conviction or merely coasting in comfort.

Life hits. The layoff comes. The diagnosis arrives. The relationship ends. And suddenly, the bench where you once nodded through sermons becomes your hiding place from God Himself. That's the moment faith gets tested. Not in the shout, but in the silence. Not in the church service, but in the courtroom. Not in the breakthrough, but in the breakdown. These slopes expose the depth—or the absence—of what was built.

No More Illusions

There is something brutally honest about hardship. It strips the soul. It silences the fluff. It separates clichés from truth. On the harsh slope, motivational memes won't sustain you. Church attendance alone won't rescue you. Singing "It Is Well" doesn't help when your world is on fire unless you've truly surrendered to the One who anchors your soul. Pain is a revealer. It shows who's climbing with a lifeline—and who's just posing for the picture.

Spiritual maturity isn't formed in comfort. It is forged in crisis. Without a safety net, every step becomes intentional. You learn to depend on the unseen rather than the comfort. You become aware of your footing—your beliefs, your disciplines, your values. The climb becomes your teacher. The slope exposes your soul.

The Risk Of Authentic Faith

Walking with God—truly walking with Him—means venturing where there are no railings. He'll call you out of the boat like Peter. He'll lead you to the wilderness like Elijah. He'll ask you to speak truth in dangerous places like Esther. Faith without risk isn't faith, it's religion. It's routine. *Real* faith requires steps that make no sense in the natural.

The problem is that many believers want safety more than surrender. We want predictable outcomes more than providential obedience. But God rarely leads through the safe route. He's not interested in coddling your comfort—He's committed to cultivating your character. That means painful detours. Unseen delays. Lonely climbs. But it's in those places where you see Him most clearly.

The Temptation To Turn Back

Every climber comes to a point where turning back seems easier than going forward. The pressure is too much. The silence is too loud. The slope is too steep. You remember the ease of sitting in the pew, clapping to the beat, giving the appearance of holiness without ever having to live it. The enemy uses exhaustion to whisper lies: "You're not strong enough." "This isn't worth it." "Just go back to normal."

But returning to the bench means surrendering your assignment. Settling for a form of godliness while denying its power. Turning back is easier—but it's also emptier. That's why God gives climbers supernatural endurance.

Isaiah 40:31 reminds us, *"But those who hope in the Lord will renew their strength. They will soar on wings like eagles; they will run and not grow weary; they will walk and not be faint."* The strength to keep going is found not in the ease of the climb but in the hope of the summit.

You Don't Climb Alone

Perhaps the most dangerous lie the enemy tells climbers is this: *"You're doing this alone."* But God has never called anyone to climb alone.

From Genesis to Revelation, His promise is the same: *"I am with you."* When Moses faced Pharaoh, God said, *"I will go with you."* When Joshua entered battle, God said, *"I will never leave you."* When Jesus ascended, He promised, *"I will be with you always."*

Even in your silent climbs, God is not absent. He is present in silence. He is whispering when the world is screaming. He is holding you when you don't feel Him. And often, He places others along the slope—mentors, pastors, spiritual friends—to remind you that you are seen. You are supported. You are not forgotten.

From Slipping To Scaling

If you've slipped on the slope, take heart. Falling isn't failure unless you choose not to rise again. David slipped into sin. Peter slipped into denial. Elijah slipped into depression. Yet all were restored. The climb isn't about perfection, it's about persistence. It's not about having all the answers—it's about trusting the One who does.

So, grip tighter. Plant your foot firmer. Whisper one more prayer. Worship one more time. You are not abandoned. You are not invisible. The harsh slopes of reality are not proof of God's absence —they are often the stage for His greatest revelation.

Your climb is your calling.

And though there may be no safety net **beneath** you, there is always a Savior **beside** you.

CHAPTER 5

THE UNMOVED MESSAGE

- Sermons That Echo But Don't Enter – Why hearing isn't the same as heeding.

- Familiarity Breeds Blindness – When truth becomes background noise.

- Spiritual Numbness– How we become desensitized to conviction.

- The Heart That Won't Yield – Walls we build against truth.

- Seeds on Shallow Ground– The parable of the sower revisited.

"They hear your words but do not put them into practice. With their mouths they express devotion, but their hearts are greedy for unjust gain."
—Ezekiel 33:31 (NIV)

Seed On Shallow Soil

Each week, sermons go forth like seed—rich with truth, pregnant with purpose. But for many, the seed never takes root. Like the parable Jesus told, the message may be heard but is quickly stolen by distraction, doubt, or hardened hearts. Too often, we listen for an emotional uplift, not life-altering revelation. The Word can't grow in hardened soil, and many hearts have grown calloused by routine and neglect.

Spiritual Amnesia

It's become a running joke—ask someone what Sunday's sermon was about on Tuesday, and most can't remember. But this isn't funny in the spirit. It's tragic. How can we live what we can't even recall?

Spiritual amnesia stems from hearing without hunger. We treat the Word like background noise, not the bread of life. When we stop valuing sermons as divine instruction, we rob ourselves of transformation.

Conviction Without Change

Conviction without application leads to callousness. We feel bad for a moment, maybe even cry during altar call—but go right back to what we were doing. The Holy Spirit convicts us not to shame us, but to change us. Yet, when we repeatedly ignore His prompts, we harden. Over time, we don't feel Him at all. Not because He left—but because we stopped listening.

The Myth Of Being "Fed"

Many blame pastors, saying "I'm not being fed." But spiritual growth isn't just the preacher's job—it's yours. We must stop expecting Sunday sermons to carry the weight of our entire walk. The pulpit isn't a spoon—it's a sword. We must open our own Bibles, chew the Word daily, and be self-feeding Christians who know how to study and apply truth on our own.

The Unlived Gospel

The gospel is not just meant to be heard—it's meant to be lived. Jesus didn't say, "Admire Me." He said, *"Follow Me."* That means our lives must reflect His character. A gospel we don't live becomes a gospel we eventually don't believe. If our lives look no different than before salvation, we must ask—did we really receive the truth, or just sit through it?

The Power Of Pretending — Playing Church While Dying Inside

The Mask That Fits Too Well

We live in an age where image trumps integrity, where performance is often praised more than purity. Nowhere is this more dangerous than in the church. There are people who show up week after week, Bible in hand, smile on their face, saying all the right things—and yet they're dying inside. They've mastered the language of the church but lost the life of Christ. They're experts at pretending, professionals at hiding. And the pew has become the perfect place to play the part.

The truth is, it's easier to put on the mask than to admit you're struggling. There's an unspoken pressure in many churches to "have it all together." Vulnerability feels risky. Honesty feels dangerous. And so, people keep quiet. They clap when everyone else claps. They nod as if they understand. They lift their hands in worship, but their hearts are heavy with secrets. They leave service encouraged by a message they never applied—and the cycle continues.

The Spiritual Exhaustion Of Living A Lie

Pretending is exhausting. It drains the soul. It's one thing to be spiritually dry. It's another way to act like you're on fire. The longer someone fakes it, the more distant they feel from the presence of God. They begin to believe that the only version of themselves God accepts is the one they perform on Sundays. But God is not looking for perfect performances. He's drawn to broken truth.

Psalm 34:18 declares, *"The Lord is close to the brokenhearted and saves those who are crushed in spirit."*

God meets us in authenticity. He moves in honesty. But when you hide behind a false version of yourself, you close the door on healing. Many are dying spiritually not because God has abandoned them, but because they're too afraid to show Him the real mess.

The Church Culture that enables pretending church culture must take responsibility for some of this. In many environments, vulnerability is punished. Confession is met with gossip. Questions are viewed as rebellion. Mental health struggles are labeled as spiritual weakness. The result? A generation of believers who have

44

learned to fake freedom because real struggles are met with religious shame.

This culture must shift.

We must create communities where it's okay to *not* be okay. Where the altar is not a place of exposure but of healing. Where leaders model transparency, not just theology. Where discipleship includes both the mountaintop and the valley. Until then, people will continue to play the part—while privately falling apart.

Jesus Never Played Pretend

Jesus never faked anything. He wept. He got angry. He bled. He asked God to "take this cup" if possible. He felt deeply, loved passionately, and lived authentically. His greatest confrontations weren't with sinners—they were with pretenders.

The Pharisees looked the part but lacked the heart. Jesus said they were like "whitewashed tombs"— beautiful on the outside but full of death inside (**Matthew 23:27**).

He didn't condemn the woman at the well or the adulteress caught in sin. He didn't shame Peter after denial or Thomas for doubting. But He consistently confronted hypocrisy. Why? Because pretending is poison. It keeps people bound while looking blessed. It keeps people in sin while shouting "Hallelujah." It keeps the church busy—but not broken, filled—but not free.

Taking Off the Mask

It takes courage to be honest. To say, *"I'm not okay."* To admit, *"I don't feel close to God."* To confess, *"I've been pretending."* Because in that honesty, healing begins.

James 5:16 encourages us, *"Confess your sins to each other and pray for each other so that you may be healed."* Healing is connected to confession. Freedom is tied to honesty.

You don't need to be perfect. You need to be real. You don't need to impress the church. You need to meet Jesus. And He doesn't require a mask—He requires your heart. The bench has waited long enough. It's time to rise, time to heal, time to be whole. Not just in appearance—but in truth.

"HEARING TRUTH WITHOUT HEEDING IT WILL LEAVE YOU SPIRITUALLY FULL... AND ETERNALLY UNCHANGED."

—Patricia S. Tanner

CHAPTER 6

THE GOSSIPING SAINTS

- Sanctified Shade—When after-church conversations become slander.

- The Tongue That Cancels Truth—Speaking life vs. speaking death.

- Parking Lot Poison—How gossip undoes what the Spirit tried to build.

- Accountability vs. Accusation—The difference between correction and criticism.

- Unity Under Fire—Fighting the enemy, not each other.

> *"The tongue has the power of life and death, and those who love it will eat its fruit."*

—Proverbs 18:21 (NIV)

The Exit-Way Disconnection

What happens in the car ride home after church says a lot about our spiritual condition. Do we reflect on what God said? Or are we immediately back to scrolling, gossiping, complaining about traffic, or critiquing the service? The enemy doesn't wait until Monday—he snatches the Word before we hit the parking lot. What we do after the benediction shows whether we came to encounter or just to observe.

The Critic Culture

We have become spiritual food critics. We rate worship. We dissect sermons. We judge church events with Yelp-style commentary. We speak more about delivery than content, about style than substance. In doing so, we've lost the fear of the Lord. The Word of God is not up for review—it's meant for reverence and obedience.

Shallow Community

The church lobby is filled with handshakes and hugs—but where's the depth? Where are the honest conversations? Where is the sharpening? Post-service talk is often surface level because vulnerability is rare. We need to build church cultures where confession, growth, and authenticity are normal—not awkward exceptions. Otherwise, we become a gathering of acquaintances instead of a family of faith.

Relational Revival

God often moves through conversation. The disciples on the road to Emmaus encountered the resurrected Jesus through dialogue. Real revival can start in the hallway, in a car ride, or at lunch after service. It won't happen if we're not listening to each other or willing to speak truth in love. We need to reimagine *"after church"* as just as sacred as *"during church."*

The Power Of Testimony

Instead of casual talk, what if we shared testimonies? What if we reminded each other of what God is doing? Faith grows by hearing—not just sermons, but stories. Testimony culture revives dying faith, unites believers, and opens hearts. Let's revive the practice of talking about Jesus more than we talk about church logistics.

The Unopened Bible —
Knowing The Word But Not Living It

Bibles In Hands, Dust On Pages

In today's world, the Bible has become more of a symbol than a sword. It rests on coffee tables, tucked into purses, quoted in captions—but rarely opened with trembling awe. We carry the Word, but do we consume it? We memorize verses, but do we embody them?

The tragedy is not just biblical illiteracy—it's spiritual indifference. People know what the Bible says but still choose their own way. The book has become decorative instead of directive. Revered but not obeyed. Quoted but not lived.

Many believers can recite Scripture they never intend to apply. They know the stories. They know the promises. They even post the verses online. But the power of the Bible isn't in the quoting—it's in the doing.

James 1:22 warns us, *"Do not merely listen to the word, and so deceive yourselves. Do what it says."* Knowing without doing is spiritual deception. And it's more common than we admit.

A Generation Dying Of Spiritual Starvation

We are spiritually malnourished in a time of biblical abundance. Never in history has the Word of God been more accessible—apps, podcasts, study plans, YouTube sermons. And yet, never has it been more neglected. We scroll for inspiration but rarely sit for instruction. We highlight verses but avoid obedience. And the soul suffers from it.

People wonder why they feel powerless, anxious, or stuck—but their Bibles stay closed. The Word is the bread of life, but we settle for crumbs from motivational memes. We wait for a Sunday message to carry us through the week, never realizing that spiritual strength is built in the daily discipline of reading and responding to God's voice. The truth is that your spiritual health is directly tied to your relationship with His Word.

Information Without Transformation

It's possible to be biblically informed but spiritually unchanged. You can study theology, attend Bible studies, and know Greek and Hebrew—and still lack love, humility, or holiness.

THE BENCH THAT WAITED

Jesus said to the Pharisees in **John 5:39-40**, *"You study the Scriptures diligently because you think that in them you have eternal life. These are the very Scriptures that testify about me, yet you refuse to come to me to have life."*

The purpose of the Bible is not head knowledge—it's heart transformation. It should lead us to Jesus. It should confront us, comfort us, and change us. But if we read it only to be right, or to defend our opinions, or to feel spiritual, then we've missed the point entirely. The Word is a mirror, not a megaphone. It's meant to show us who we are—not just who others should be.

Excuses We Love To Use

"I don't understand it."

"I don't have time."

"I'll get serious next season."

These are the phrases of delayed obedience and delayed obedience is still disobedience. God never said you must master every verse. He said you must seek Him with your whole heart. Start small. Be consistent. Invite the Holy Spirit to illuminate what you don't understand. Make time—not excuses. Your life depends on it.

The Word is alive.

Hebrews 4:12 declares, *"For the word of God is alive and active. Sharper than any double-edged sword..."* It cuts. It heals. It exposes. It awakens. But it cannot do any of that if it stays closed. An unopened Bible is like an unopened letter from God—waiting, full of truth, ignored.

From Head To Heart To Habit

Transformation begins when we move beyond memorization to meditation, beyond study to surrender. Reading Scripture should be relational, not just informational. Ask, *"God, what are You saying to me?" "Where am I out of alignment?" "How can I obey this today?"*

Apply the Word even when it's uncomfortable. Forgive because it's commanded. Love because it's written. Give because it's truth. Stand because it's righteousness. Let the Word become flesh in your life. Let it shape your thoughts, your actions, your relationships. The goal isn't just to know more verses—it's to become more like Jesus.

The unopened Bible is a tragedy not because it lacks power, but because we've forgotten how desperately we need it. Don't just carry it—consume it. Don't just quote it—live it. Don't just hear it—do it.

The bench has waited long enough.

Let the pages turn.

Let the Word speak. And let your life respond.

CHAPTER 7

THE
FORM OF
GODLINESS

• Church Culture Over Kingdom Character—Putting tradition above transformation.

• Checklists of Righteousness—Mistaking religious acts for righteous living.

• Rules Without Relationship—Legalism's grip on modern faith.

• The Idol of Attendance—Believing presence equals power.

• The Power We Deny—What happens when the Holy Spirit is silenced.

"Having a form of godliness but denying its power. Have nothing to do with such people."

—2 Timothy 3:5 (NIV)

Silent Tears Of The Spirit

There's a soundlessness to spiritual decay. People cry inwardly while smiling outwardly. The bench often holds tears no one sees— tears of people tired of pretending, tired of performance, and tired of being spiritually paralyzed. Their souls ache, but because they're in church, they feel pressured to appear okay. These are the weeping benches—where silent breakdowns are disguised behind loud hallelujahs.

The Unseen Struggle

Many are battling depression, addiction, identity crises, and trauma while attending every church service. But no one knows. The church has unintentionally created a culture where pain is hidden, not healed. The fear of judgment silences the wounded, who end up crying into pews instead of crying out for help. These benches know the weight of unseen burdens.

The Danger Of Isolation In A Crowd

It's possible to feel alone in a room full of believers. We clap together but suffer alone. The bench is often where people bury their emotions. They come hoping someone will notice, ask, or care—but leave untouched. The body of Christ must reawaken its sensitivity.

THE BENCH THAT WAITED

We cannot allow people to spiritually bleed while surrounded by the solution.

When Worship Becomes A Mask

Some use worship to hide instead of healing. They shout the loudest to cover their silence. They dance to forget, not to overcome. The bench watches them, week after week, knowing the difference between performance and pursuit. God wants worship that heals, not hides. He wants His people to bring their brokenness—not their best mask.

Healing Begins With Honesty

The bench that once held silent tears can become the altar of breakthrough if honesty is allowed. Healing in the church begins when people feel safe to say, *"I'm not okay."* We must shift from pretending to presence—from impressing to confessing. Only then can God move through the community to restore the weary and bind up the brokenhearted.

The Silent Tears Of The Spiritually Numb.

There's a deep ache that sits in the soul of a person who used to feel God—who used to hear Him, sense Him, respond to Him—but now finds only silence. No fire. No tears. No stirring in worship. Just a numbness that clings like fog.

These are not unbelievers. These are the ones who once danced at the altar. The ones who prayed until they lost track of time. Now they sit, unmoved, uncertain, and unnoticed. These are the weeping benches. Silent. Still. But screaming from within.

Spiritual numbness is the slow death of the soul's sensitivity. It's not always caused by sin. Sometimes it's exhaustion. Sometimes it's pain. Sometimes it's an overload of unanswered prayers. It creeps in subtly—first in a missed morning prayer, then in a skipped devotion, then in disconnected worship. Over time, the vibrant connection to God begins to dull until you can't feel Him anymore. And that terrifies you, but you don't know how to say it out loud.

Tears That No One Sees

You still go to church. Still serve. Still smile. But inside, something is off. You want to feel again, but you're afraid the tears, once they start, won't stop. You want to scream, but no one has given you permission to break.

The bench is your hiding place. And though you look composed, your spirit weeps in silence. *"Why can't I feel You, God?"* becomes your silent prayer. **Psalm 42:3** captures this heartbreak: *"My tears have been my food day and night, while people say to me all day long, 'Where is your God?'"*

Spiritual numbness is isolating. It feels like you're the only one who's dry. Everyone else seems "on fire," lifting hands and shouting amen. You wonder if something's wrong with *you*. But you're not alone. Elijah once asked God to take his life. David cried out in the Psalms for God not to hide His face. Even Jesus, in His humanity, groaned in the garden, feeling abandoned. If the greats of faith walked through numbness, why do we think we must *always* feel okay?

The Hidden Causes Of Numbness

Sometimes spiritual numbness is the body's emotional survival response to trauma. When you've endured loss, betrayal, church hurt, or personal disappointment, the soul can shut down in self-protection. Other times, numbness is caused by burnout—doing for

God without being *with* God. When you're always pouring out and never being poured into, eventually the well runs dry.

It can also come from sin—not just the sin of rebellion, but the sin of neglect. Ignoring conviction. Delaying obedience. Living in spiritual apathy. The longer we suppress the Spirit's whisper, the fainter it becomes. Eventually, our heart builds callouses. And what once made us weep now barely makes us blink.

When The Weeping Bench Becomes Sacred

But here's the hope: numbness is not death. It's a sign that the soul is still alive, still fighting to feel. And sometimes, it's in the weeping that the Spirit whispers loudest.

Psalm 56:8 reminds us, *"You keep track of all my sorrows. You have collected all my tears in your bottle."* Not one tear shed in silence is wasted.

God is not repelled by your numbness—He's drawn to it. He meets you at the bench. He sits in silence. He speaks through the dryness. You may not feel Him, but He is not absent. Feelings are not the measure of faith. Obedience is. Keep showing up. Keep reading. Keep praying. Keep worshiping. Even when you feel nothing. That consistency becomes a declaration: "I may not feel You, but I still choose You."

The Way Back To Feeling

Healing begins with honesty. Tell God you feel nothing. He already knows. Be real in your prayers. Ask Him to awaken your heart. Then remove the noise. Fast from distractions. Rest. Find a safe space to cry. Find someone to talk to. Surround yourself with people who won't just hype you but help you.

The return to feeling is not always instant. Sometimes it's gradual. Like thawing ice. A moment in worship breaks something. A verse finally hits home. A dream reignites. A single tear falls during prayer. That's how the bench stops weeping—when the heart starts feeling again.

Don't fear your numbness. It's often the place where God is softening you for something deeper. Don't fake passion. Ask for fire.

Don't pretend to be okay.

Let the bench hold your truth.

When God visits you again—and He will—you'll remember that even when you felt nothing, He will turn your heart of stone into a heart of flesh.

"YOU CAN MASTER THE FORM AND STILL MISS THE FIRE. GOD NEVER CALLED US TO ACT HOLY—HE CALLED US TO BE."

—Patricia S. Tanner

CHAPTER 8

THE FELLOWSHIP ILLUSION

• More Than Church Friends-Friendly without being for real.

• Clapping Together–Crumbling Apart-Corporate praise while quietly breaking.

• Dressed For Church–Undressed Before God-Giving the mirror more time than God.

• The Idol Of Image- When appearance is more important than God.

• Trading Costumes For Crosses-Chase authenticity, not applause.

"They honor me with their lips, but their hearts are far from me."
—Mark 7:6b (NIV)

More Than Church Friends

We've mastered the art of being friendly without being real. Many church connections stop at greetings, shared service duties, or small talk after Sunday service.

True fellowship goes deeper—it bears burdens, speaks truth, and builds trust. Without this depth, our "community" is just proximity with religious vocabulary.

Loneliness In The Midst Of Many

The tragedy of the modern church is that you can know everyone and still feel known by no one. Real fellowship is intentional. It asks hard questions, listens without judgment, and doesn't disappear during trials. The illusion of fellowship is the assumption that shared beliefs equal shared lives.

Clapping Together, Crumbling Apart

We praise corporately but often break privately. Worship unites us in sound but not always in spirit. Many feel isolated while performing unity. This is why the early church in Acts was so powerful—they didn't just worship together, they lived together. They shared their lives, resources, struggles, and victories.

The Fear Of Being Known

Authentic fellowship demands vulnerability, and that scares people. We fear being judged, exposed, or rejected. But we must risk being seen to be healed. The fellowship illusion dies when we choose honesty over image, truth over reputation, and depth over surface connection.

Discipleship Over Friendship

Fellowship must lead to discipleship. It's not enough to hang out, we must help each other grow. A true friend in Christ doesn't just encourage—they correct, guide, and sharpen. The goal is not popularity in church, but purity in purpose. A community of disciples is what the church was always meant to be.

The Fashion Show Of Faith — When Appearance Replaces Transformation

Dressed For Church, Undressed Before God

It's Sunday morning.

The outfit is picked out the night before. Shoes polished. Wig laid. Beard trimmed. The mirror gets more attention than the mirror of God's Word. We arrive ready to be seen, but not necessarily ready to be changed. This is the fashion show of faith—a spiritual masquerade where the wardrobe screams worship but the heart stays hidden. And sadly, many have mastered the art of looking saved without living surrendered.

Appearance has become a currency in church culture. Social media is flooded with 'Sunday best' selfies captioned with Bible verses that aren't practiced. We've turned sanctuaries into runways. Holiness has become an aesthetic. We quote "Come as you are," but dress to impress. We gather in God's name but posture for people's approval. And all the while, God is whispering, *"I don't want your garments—I want your heart."*

The Idol Of Image

There is nothing inherently wrong with dressing well. God is not anti-fashion. He clothed the lilies of the field with splendor. But when appearance becomes the priority, and when transformation becomes optional, we've created a counterfeit gospel. The idol of image thrives in environments where surface-level faith is celebrated more than surrendered lives.

This issue is not new.

In **Matthew 23:5**, Jesus called out the Pharisees, saying, *"Everything they do is done for people to see: They make their phylacteries wide and the tassels on their garments long."* They looked righteous, but their hearts were far from God. He wasn't impressed by their spiritual couture. He wanted their confession, their brokenness, their obedience.

When Performance Replaces Presence

We've become skilled at performing faith—knowing when to shout, how to nod, when to lift our hands. Church services can sometimes feel more like productions than places of presence. And tragically, some don't know the difference. The presence of God becomes a 'vibe' instead of a divine encounter.

You can sing on key and still be out of alignment with God. You can cry on cue and still harbor bitterness. You can lead worship and still lust in your heart. This is why Scripture says in **2 Timothy 3:5**, *"They will act religious, but they will reject the power that could make them godly."*

Image is easy.

Transformation is costly.

THE BENCH THAT WAITED

Church Hurt vs. Self-Deception

Many blame the church for being judgmental. And yes, religious pride can be toxic. But sometimes the real issue isn't the judgment of others, it's the shame we carry from knowing we're pretending. We dress up to hide our dysfunction. We worship louder to drown out conviction. We volunteer more to overcompensate for the areas we refuse to surrender. And when no one calls us out, we confuse silence with approval.

But God sees through the fabric.

Isaiah 64:6 says, *"All our righteous acts are like filthy rags."* In other words, no matter how dressed up we look to others, God knows what's underneath. He is not impressed by our performance. He is drawn to our repentance. He will not bless what we pretend to be. He blesses who we are willing to become.

Trading Costumes For Crosses

It's time to take off the costume. Lay down the pretense. Stop chasing applause and start chasing authenticity. Following Jesus is not about curated perfection. It's about daily surrender. About letting the Word cut where it must. It's about allowing the Spirit to refine what pride wants to protect.

Transformation happens when we stop hiding and start healing. When we admit we don't have it all together. When we stop performing and start repenting. When we take off the polished persona and bring God our raw, real selves. That's when breakthrough happens. That's when chains fall. That's when revival starts—not in our wardrobes, but in our hearts.

So next time you get dressed for church, pause. Look deeper.

Ask: *"Am I ready to be seen by God more than I want to be seen by others?"*

Let your faith be more than a fashion statement.

Let it be a life-altering transformation.

"YOU CAN'T HEAL WHAT YOU HIDE. OFFENSE IS A PRISON DISGUISED AS PROTECTION."

—Patricia S. Tanner

CHAPTER 9

THE GOSPEL OF CONVENIENCE

• Jesus as an Emergency Exit–When Jesus should be a way of life.

• Selective Obedience–We obey when it's convenient.

• Church Without The Cross–The gospel without the cross is powerless.

• Position Without Purity–Know that the Lord looks at the heart.

• When Conviction Is Silenced By Approval.

"Whoever wants to be my disciple must deny themselves and take up their cross daily and follow me."

—Luke 9:23 (NIV)

Jesus As An Emergency Exit

Many treat God like a 911 call—only needed in crisis. The gospel becomes a backup plan, not a way of life. This mindset breeds consumer Christianity: "What can God do for me?" rather than "How can I serve Him?" When faith is built on convenience, it collapses under conviction.

Selective Obedience

We obey when it's easy, comfortable, or beneficial. But Jesus calls us to deny ourselves—not indulge selectively. The gospel is not about fitting God into our schedule; it's about surrendering our lives entirely. We can't cherry-pick the commandments we like and ignore the ones that cost us something.

Blessings Without Lordship

Everyone wants the blessings of God—healing, provision, favor— but few want His Lordship. Jesus is more than a miracle worker; He is King. To call Him Lord means our lives are no longer our own. The gospel of convenience promotes comfort, but the Kingdom calls us to commitment.

Church Without The Cross

Modern messages often avoid talk about suffering, sacrifice, or sin. The cross is uncomfortable, so we edit it out. But without the cross, there is no Christianity. The gospel without the cross is powerless. We need preaching that pierces, not just pampers—truth that transforms, not just entertains.

Comfort Is Not The Goal

Jesus never promised comfort—He promised a cross. The gospel demands everything but gives even more. If our faith never confronts us, stretches us, or costs us, then it's not the gospel of Jesus Christ. We must reject the diluted version of Christianity that centers us instead of Christ.

The Pastor's Pet —
Hiding in Favor While Ignoring Conviction

The Blessing That Blinds

There's a dangerous comfort that comes from being close to the pulpit. When you're favored by the pastor, constantly affirmed, celebrated for your loyalty, or given positions of influence, it's easy to mistake favor for spiritual health. You begin to believe you're doing well because you're visible. You assume you're right with God because you're right with leadership. But favor with man doesn't always equal favor with God.

Many "Pastor's Pets" unknowingly fall into a spiritual slumber. They've confused affirmation for accountability. They've replaced conviction with compliments. And the applause of their leader has dulled their sensitivity to the Holy Spirit. In this position, correction becomes rare. Rebuke becomes offensive. And transformation becomes optional.

Position Without Purity

Being elevated in a church setting without inner transformation can be one of the most deceptive experiences in the faith. When you have access to the stage but not to a surrendered life, you become a performance artist instead of a disciple. You know how to say the right things. You know what scriptures to quote. But behind the scenes, there's a private struggle, an unaddressed sin, or a growing pride that no one confronts.

1 Samuel 16:7 reminds us, *"People look at the outward appearance, but the Lord looks at the heart."* Saul had favor with Israel, but God had rejected him long before anyone else knew. Judas walked closely with Jesus but never allowed his heart to be transformed. Proximity to leadership is not the same as intimacy with God.

When Conviction Is Silenced By Approval

The danger of always being praised is that you begin to silence the still, small voice that convicts. You start ignoring red flags in your heart. You downplay your attitude. You justify your bitterness. You suppress your struggle. After all, if the pastor isn't concerned, why should you be?

But God is not obligated to speak through popularity. He speaks through truth. And truth often wounds before it heals. **Hebrews 12:6** says, *"The Lord disciplines the one He loves."* If you haven't been corrected in a while, it might be because you've surrounded yourself with comfort instead of conviction.

Manipulating Leadership For Approval

There's another layer to the Pastor's Pet syndrome— manipulation. Some individuals learn how to say exactly what a leader wants to hear. They flatter, perform, and imitate submission. But beneath it is a strategic attempt to maintain favor while avoiding true accountability. This is spiritual politics, and it's dangerous.

It creates cliques within churches, fosters jealousy among the body, and builds platforms on personal preference rather than spiritual maturity.

Proverbs 29:5 warns, *"Those who flatter their neighbors are spreading nets for their feet."* When you live off affirmation, your faith becomes fragile—dependent on applause rather than anchored in truth.

From Pet To Servant

The goal isn't to be the favorite, it's to be faithful. To be known by God, not just celebrated by man. To welcome correction. To seek conviction. To desire growth more than applause. True servants of God understand that honor is a byproduct of holiness, not a substitute for it.

Ask yourself: if your pastor never affirmed you again, would you still serve? If no one clapped for you, would you still obey? If your title was removed, would you still pursue God with passion? These are the questions that reveal your motives. Don't live for favor. Live for faithfulness.

Let your heart remain tender.

Let your ears stay open to correction. Let your life reflect the truth of God's Word, not just the praise of man. Because when the applause fades and the spotlight dims, only one thing matters—did you hear *"Well done"* from the One who matters most?

"THERE'S NOTHING MORE TRAGIC THAN A FULL BENCH AND AN EMPTY PURPOSE. DON'T LET YOUR DESTINY DIE WAITING ON YOUR PERMISSION TO BEGIN."

-Patricia S. Tanner

CHAPTER 10

❧

ATTENDANCE DOES NOT EQUAL ASSIGNMENT

• Showing Up Without Showing Out-Don't confuse being present with being positioned.

• Discipleship is the Assignment-He called us to be disciples.

• Find Your Function-The bench is not your home.

• From Spectator to Participant-You should chase transformation.

• What the Bench Has Cost You-Don't lose your fire.

"Why do you call me, 'Lord, Lord,' and do not do what I say?"
—Luke 6:46 (NIV)

Showing Up Without Showing Out

Faithful attendance at church is commendable, but it's not the same as fulfilling your spiritual assignment. Many believers confuse being present with being positioned. They assume that because they are in the room, they're also in God's will. But merely showing up every Sunday is not a substitute for showing out in obedience, service, and spiritual growth.

The Kingdom of God moves through active vessels—not passive pew-sitters. Your assignment was never to just warm a bench—it was to carry the fire beyond the altar.

The Myth Of Spiritual Proximity

Just because you're near the presence of God doesn't mean you're aligned with it. Judas sat beside Jesus, but his heart was far from Him. Likewise, thousands gather in church buildings weekly but remain unaligned with their purpose. The enemy doesn't mind if you sit in church every week—if you never become who God called you to be. Proximity to God's house doesn't always mean transformation in God's Kingdom.

Discipleship Is The Assignment

Jesus didn't call us to be churchgoers—He called us to be disciples. That means transformation, surrender, and spiritual multiplication. Being a disciple means you're not just consuming spiritual content—you're living it, sharing it, and helping others grow in it. The great commission was not "Go and sit in all the nations," but *"Go and make disciples."* Our assignment is action-based, not attendance-based.

From Spectator To Servant

The church has too many spectators and not enough servants. Spectators critique the worship, the preaching, the people—but servants ask, "Where can I help? Who can I serve?" There's a joy and purpose that only comes from stepping into your calling. Sitting may feel safe, but serving is where the anointing flows. There's no such thing as a 'benched believer' in the Kingdom.

Everyone has a role—are you playing yours?

Find Your Function

Every believer has a gift, and every gift has a place in God's Kingdom. You weren't saved to sit—you were saved to serve. Some are called to teach, others to intercede, encourage, build, write, create, lead, or nurture. The key is to find your function and walk in it fully. The longer you stay on the bench, the more you rob the world of the healing your obedience could bring.

The Bench That Waited —
A Final Invitation to Get Up and Walk in Truth

The Bench Is Not Your Home There is a sacred stillness in every sanctuary—a quiet place near the back where so many hearts have sat. The bench. A place of comfort, but also a place of delay. For some, it was a place to catch their breath. For others, it became a place to hide. The bench waited. Patiently. Week after week. Year after year.

As the message went forth, while the Spirit moved, while others answered the altar call, the bench quietly held its occupant, waiting for a decision that never came.

This chapter is not about judgment. It's about the invitation. An invitation to get up. To move. To live. Because while God's grace will sit with you on the bench, His calling will not leave you there. You were not saved to be still. You were not filled to be silent. There comes a point where the bench, once a place of healing, can become a place of spiritual paralysis.

From Spectator To Participant

Far too many have grown comfortable spectating the move of God. Watching others be healed. Watching others grow. Watching others preach, sing, serve, and lead. And yet never asking themselves: *"Why not me?"* We have a generation of believers who clap for transformation but never chase it. Who amen the truth but never apply it.

James 1:22 says, *"Do not merely listen to the word, and so deceive yourselves. Do what it says."*

Obedience is the bridge from faith to fruit. It's not enough to agree with the sermon. It's not enough to nod in service. God is calling you to live what you've heard—to rise from the bench and engage your faith.

What The Bench Has Cost You

Some have sat so long on the bench that their dreams have dust on them. Their identity has grown blurry. Their fire has gone out. You once felt called to lead worship. You once felt pulled to teach or preach, to create or serve—but fear, comfort, or self- doubt kept you seated. The longer you sit, the easier it becomes to convince yourself that it's too late.

But **Romans 11:29** reminds us, *"For the gifts and the calling of God are irrevocable."* That means it's not too late. The bench does not cancel your calling—it simply delays your response. And delay can be dangerous. Some opportunities have windows. Some doors will not stay open forever. Get up while there's still time.

When The Bench Becomes A Crutch

There are times when God allows a bench season. Moments where rest is holy. Where healing is needed. Where stillness is strategic. But what begins as a season can become a sentence if you refuse to move forward. The enemy doesn't always use sin to stop you— sometimes he just convinces you to stay put.

The Spirit is prompting you to forgive, but the bench says, *"Just wait a little longer."* The Spirit nudges you to pray for someone, but the bench says, "Let someone else do it." The Spirit is stirring you to start the ministry, to confront the addiction, to apologize to the family member— but the bench has lulled you into spiritual sleep.

The Call To Rise

Jesus often spoke with one phrase that shook people to their core: *"Get up."* To the lame man, to the sleeping child, to the man at the pool of Bethesda, He said, *"Get up and walk."* There was no long speech. Just an invitation to move. And today, that same call echoes through the sanctuary of your soul.

Get up from shame. Get up from pride. Get up from fear. Get up from cycles. Get up from excuses. The bench has waited long enough. Your destiny is not tied to comfort—it's tied to courage.

The Kingdom needs your voice, your story, your gifts. Your family needs your healing. Your generation needs your obedience.

Isaiah 60:1 declares, *"Arise, shine, for your light has come, and the glory of the Lord rises upon you."* This is the moment. The turning point. The final invitation. The bench won't stop you. But you must stop sitting.

Let this be the chapter that moves you from watching to walking. From silence to surrender. From stuck to sent. Get up. Walk in truth. And never return to the bench that waited.

"HE DIDN'T WAIT FOR THE ALTAR CALL—HE SAT NEXT TO YOU IN THE PEW. JESUS HAS ALWAYS BEEN CLOSER THAN WE PRETENDED TO NOTICE."

—Patricia S. Tanner

CHAPTER 11

❧⟡❧

THE IDOL
OF CHURCH
CULTURE

• The Brand of Belief- Church has become a brand.

• Popularity in the Pulpit-Pastors have become celebrities.

• The Role You've Learned to Play-Many perfect the role of a believer.

• The Danger of Spiritual Performance-Don't impress people, move God.

• The Price of Pretending-Counterfeit Christianity comes with a cost.

"These people come near to me with their mouth and honor me with their lips, but their hearts are far from me. Their worship of me is based merely on human rules they have been taught."
—Isaiah 29:13 (NIV*)***

The Brand Of Belief

Church has become a brand in many places—a place of aesthetics and influence, rather than depth and repentance. We've created logos, playlists, hashtags, and merchandise—but often lost the raw power of deliverance and devotion.

When culture overtakes calling, we stop building altars and start building platforms. The church is not a club, it's a covenant community built around the cross, not convenience.

Programs Over Presence

A packed church calendar doesn't mean we're doing God's will. Busyness can become a barrier to intimacy with Christ. We run events, workshops, retreats—but are we making room for the Holy Spirit? Are we planning more than we're praying? The presence of God cannot be scheduled; it must be invited, welcomed, and honored. Without His presence, we're just hosting religious events with no eternal fruit.

Popularity In The Pulpit

There's a rising trend of personality-driven churches where pastors become celebrities and spiritual authority is replaced by performance. When popularity becomes more important than purity, people starve spiritually. Leaders must point people to Christ, not themselves. 'Church culture' must be centered on Jesus—not a brand, not a following, not an influencer. The greatest among us must still be servants.

Conforming Instead Of Transforming

Too often, churches conform to society to appear "relevant." But Jesus never compromised the truth to attract crowds. The gospel is countercultural, confrontational, and holy. If we water it down to fit in, we strip it of its power. We are called to be salt and light—not echoes of culture. Church culture must transform lives, not reflect the world's broken systems in a polished package.

Recovering The Remnant

There is still a remnant—a group of believers who hunger for the real, raw, and righteous move of God. They're not impressed by production—they long for presence. They don't want entertainment, they want encounters. These are the ones God will use to rebuild altars, tear down idols, and bring revival. Church culture must shift from convenience to consecration if we are to see the glory return.

The Counterfeit Christian —
Looking The Part, Losing The Purpose

The Role You've Learned To Play

In every church, there are those who have perfected the role of the believer. They know how to shout "Hallelujah" at the right moment. They can recite scripture and quote sermons. They know how to dress, how to greet, how to appear engaged in worship—and yet behind the façade, their spiritual walk is empty. This is the dilemma of the counterfeit Christian: looking like the real thing but walking in emptiness, wearing the uniform of faith without possessing the heart of transformation.

Counterfeit Christianity is not just a lie to others—it becomes a trap for self. You start believing the image you've created. You fool yourself into thinking performance equals relationship. But deep down, you know. You know the Word doesn't convict you like it used to. You know the altar call stirs discomfort, not desire. You know your obedience is delayed, your worship rehearsed.

And God knows too.

The Danger Of Spiritual Performance

Matthew 15:8 echoes like a thunderclap: *"These people honor me with their lips, but their hearts are far from me."* Jesus saw through the image. He exposed the empty routines of the Pharisees, not to shame them, but to awaken them. Because the greatest deception isn't lying to others—it's lying to yourself.

Spiritual performance may impress people, but it does not move God. He is not persuaded by our display. He is drawn to our brokenness.

Psalm 51:17 reminds us, *"The sacrifices of God are a broken spirit; a broken and contrite heart you, God, will not despise."* There is no power in pretending. There is no breakthrough in being polished. Only the real you can be transformed.

The Exhaustion Of Faking It

Living a double life is draining. You smile, but it's forced. You serve, but you're empty. You sing, but your heart is tired. And slowly, the cracks begin to show. The anger you suppress leaks out in gossip. The insecurity festers into bitterness. The unconfessed sin grows into shame. And no matter how much you cover it up, you begin to feel like a fraud.

But God never called you to be perfect—He called you to be honest. To bring your mess, not your mask. To confess your weakness, not conceal it. He would rather meet the real you than bless the fake you. The sooner you stop performing, the sooner healing can begin.

The Price Of Pretending

Counterfeit Christianity costs more than we think. It cheapens the gospel. It confuses new believers. It hardens our own hearts. When people witness hypocrisy in the pews, they begin to distrust the message. When your children see you shouting in church but cursing at home, they question the truth. When your private life contradicts your public faith, the witness of Christ is diluted.

Jesus said in **Revelation 3:15–16**, *"I know your deeds, that you are neither cold nor hot. I wish you were either one or the other! So, because you are lukewarm... I am about to spit you out of my mouth."* God would rather you be real in your struggle than fake in your strength. He desires relationship over routine.

Returning To Authentic Faith

It's not too late. The mask can come off. The show can end. You don't need to be perfect—you just need to be real. Real repentance. Real surrender. Real growth. God is not waiting for you to act holy; He's waiting for you to become whole.

Return to your first love. Let the Word pierce again. Let worship undo you. Let the Holy Spirit lead you back into truth. You may have played a role, but now it's time to embrace the relationship.

Don't settle for the appearance of faith. Press into the authenticity of it.

The world doesn't need more performers—it needs more people willing to live the gospel out loud.

"OBEDIENCE IS NOT IN WHAT YOU HEAR—IT'S IN HOW YOU MOVE. THE MIRACLE WAS NEVER IN THE SITTING; IT WAS IN THE GETTING UP."

— Patricia S. Tanner

CHAPTER 12

KINGDOM OVER CROWD

- The Difference Between Crowd and Kingdom-Kingdom citizens follow mandates.

- Raising Sons, Not Just Spectators-God doesn't want religious robots.

- The Return of the King's Agenda-He came to establish a Kingdom.

- Anointed but Asleep-The church has become a place of tragedy.

- Burying What God Gave You-The danger of unused talents.

"But seek first the Kingdom of God and His righteousness, and all these things shall be added to you."

—Matthew 6:33 (NKJV)

The Difference Between Crowd And Kingdom

Crowds follow miracles; Kingdom citizens follow mandates. Jesus never trusted the crowds because they were fickle. One moment they praised Him; the next they cried *"Crucify Him."* Kingdom living isn't about how many people fill the sanctuary—it's about how many people walk in surrender. We must stop measuring success by numbers and start measuring it by fruit.

Kingdom Requires Accountability

In the Kingdom, you don't just get to do what you want. There's order, correction, growth, and submission to God's will. Many flee accountability because they want to stay comfortable. But the Kingdom is about growth, not comfort. True leaders won't let you stay the same—they will challenge you to become who God designed you to be.

Raising Sons, Not Just Spectators

The Kingdom is about sonship. God doesn't want religious robots— He wants sons and daughters who reflect His image and represent Him on earth. Church must transition from raising attendees to raising ambassadors. That means identity, inheritance, and spiritual authority. A Kingdom mindset teaches people not just how to sit in church—but how to reign in life through Christ.

The Cross Is The Entrance

You can't enter the Kingdom without going through the cross. There is no shortcut. Salvation is free, but discipleship will cost you everything. The Kingdom is not built on preference but on sacrifice. We must preach the cross again—not just the blessings of the Kingdom, but the blood that purchased it. The cross is where sin dies, and new life begins.

The Return Of The King's Agenda

Jesus didn't come to start a religion—He came to establish a Kingdom. That Kingdom is not Republican or Democrat. It is not Western or Eastern. It is not defined by buildings, but by believers who carry His glory. The return of Christ won't be for a church full of crowds, but for a bride prepared, pure, and positioned. It's time to put away church games and return to the King's agenda.

Chosen But Comfortable — The Trap Of Unused Potential

Anointed But Asleep

Many are called. Many are gifted. Many are chosen. But many are also comfortable. There is a tragedy unfolding across churches where anointed people have fallen asleep in their calling. They are not in sin—they are in slumber. They have not abandoned God— they have simply stopped advancing. The fire has faded into familiarity, and what once was a passionate pursuit has become a passive routine.

The trap of unused potential isn't always rebellion—it's often comfort. You serve when convenient. You give when it's easy. You pray when it's urgent. But you no longer stretch. You no longer risk.

You no longer grow. And slowly, the oil leaks from your lamp. **Matthew 25** tells the parable of the ten virgins—five wise, five foolish. The foolish were not wicked. They were unprepared. Chosen, yes—but careless with their assignment.

The Comfort Of Complacency

Complacency is seductive. It tells you that what you've done is enough. It whispers that rest is your reward, even if you haven't run the race. It convinces you that presence is participation. But spiritual laziness often wears the mask of contentment. You show up, but you no longer pour out. You listen, but you no longer respond. You nod in agreement, but conviction no longer grips you.

Hebrews 6:12 warns us not to become *"lazy, but to imitate those who through faith and patience inherit what has been promised."* God does not reward comfort—He responds to hunger. And potential that is never pursued becomes purpose that is never fulfilled.

Burying What God Gave You

In **Matthew 25:14–30**, Jesus tells the parable of the talents. One man buried his gift. He did not misuse it. He did not worship idols. He simply buried what was placed in his hands. And for that, he was called wicked and lazy. This is sobering. To bury your gift out of fear or laziness is to reject the very trust God placed in you.

Some of us were meant to lead but remain hidden. Some were called to teach but stay silent. Others were given creativity, wisdom, and vision—but postpone obedience. The bench isn't your prison anymore—your comfort zone is. But what if your next breakthrough is locked inside your next step?

THE BENCH THAT WAITED

God Requires A Return

God is an investor. He gives gifts expecting a return—not for His benefit, but for your growth and the benefit of others. **Romans 12:6** says, *"We have different gifts, according to the grace given to each of us."* That means every believer has something to bring to the table. The question is not whether you're gifted. The question is whether you're using it.

You will be held accountable not just for what you did wrong, but for what you refused to do right. For the words you never spoke. For the hands you never laid. For the books you never wrote. For the ministries you never launched. For the forgiveness you never gave. For the risks you never took.

It's Time To Move

If you feel called—move. If you feel convicted—repent. If you feel the stirring—obey. Don't wait for the perfect moment. Don't wait for another confirmation. You already have a green light from God. The potential is in you, but the permission has already been given. God's not waiting to anoint you—He's waiting for you to move.

The world doesn't need more perfect Christians. It needs willing ones. The ones who wake up. The ones who shake off comfort. The ones who say, *"I don't have it all together, but I refuse to bury what God gave me."*

You've been chosen. But chosen doesn't mean finished. There's still more in you. Don't die full. Don't waste what cost Jesus everything to give you. Rise. Step. Serve. Build. Speak. Love. Lead. Your potential is not for display—it's for deployment.

"KINGDOM ISN'T ABOUT FINDING A SEAT—IT'S ABOUT FINDING YOUR SERVICE. YOU WERE NEVER MEANT TO BE A BENCH WARMER IN THE BODY OF CHRIST."

—Patricia S. Tanner

CHAPTER 13

BENCH WARMERS AND HEART WANDERERS

• Comfort Without Conviction-The heart wanders while the body remains seated.

• The Cost Of Spiritual Indifference-Familiarity breeds contempt.

• Reviving the Fire-Don't remain a wanderer.

• The Tragedy of Tailored Truth-Sermons are trimmed to avoid offense.

• A Generation Unfazed by God-We've exchanged repentance for relevance.

The righteous shall flourish like the palm tree: he shall grow like a cedar in Lebanon....

-Psalm 92:12

Comfort Without Conviction

Some remain on the bench not out of rebellion, but out of comfort. They aren't against God—they're just not compelled enough to pursue Him deeply.

It's easier to sit through a sermon than to submit to its demands. The heart wanders while the body remains seated. This spiritual passivity has lulled many into thinking they're okay simply because they're present. But comfort without conviction is the slow death of passion.

The Cost Of Spiritual Indifference

When we grow indifferent to God's Word, it loses its transforming power in our lives. Familiarity breeds contempt, and we start to tune out the very messages that once stirred us. We hear the truth but don't tremble. We sing but don't surrender.

Indifference is dangerous because it masks itself as peace. But peace with no pursuit of righteousness is spiritual sedation.

Living Without A Sense Of Urgency

Time is not promised. Yet, many live like they have unlimited chances to get it right. The bench becomes a place of delay, but God is calling for urgency. Souls are perishing. Families are breaking.

Generations are waiting for your obedience. We can't afford to keep waiting for the "right time." God needs active hearts, not idle bodies.

The Slow Drift From Purpose

You rarely notice when you're drifting—until you look up and realize how far you are from shore. The same is true spiritually. One missed prayer becomes a week. One unchecked thought becomes a stronghold. Before long, your heart is in another country while your body still attends church. Drifting happens when we stop rowing. Purpose requires paddling—even against the current.

Reviving The Fire

The same God who called Peter back after denial still calls your name from the shore. You don't have to stay a wanderer. Revival begins when honesty returns. When you admit your drift, your doubt, your dryness. God honors a broken spirit. The bench doesn't have to be your prison—it can be your launching pad back into purpose.

The Silent Sanctuary —
Where Conviction No Longer Echoes

Muted Altars and Empty Echoes

There once was a time when the sanctuary was alive with conviction—when a single word could cut through pretense like a blade of truth. When the altar was a place of tears and trembling, not selfies and schedules. But now, in many places, silence reigns. Not the holy kind of silence, but the uncomfortable quiet that comes from avoidance. We have filled our services with sound systems but emptied them of spiritual soundness. We've muted conviction in the name of comfort.

The sanctuary has become a stage. Worship is polished. Preaching is palatable. Prayer is programmed. And the Holy Spirit is politely asked not to disrupt. But the absence of conviction is not the presence of peace, it's the symptom of a heart that's no longer listening. When the Word no longer confronts us, we're no longer growing. When it becomes entertainment, not encounter, we've left the path.

The Tragedy Of Tailored Truth

Today's church culture often tailors truth to be more marketable. Sermons are trimmed to avoid offense. Hard scriptures are skipped. Topics like sin, repentance, holiness, or hell are rarely addressed. Why? Because conviction doesn't get shared on social media. It doesn't trend. It doesn't sell books or boost attendance.

But **2 Timothy 4:3** warns us: *"For the time will come when people will not put up with sound doctrine. Instead, to suit their own desires, they will gather... teachers to say what their itching ears want to hear."*

We are in that time now. And the result is a generation that feels good but isn't transformed. They're informed but not converted. Stirred but not surrendered.

A Generation Unfazed By God

We are raising a generation who can shout in church but sin without sorrow. Who post scripture but live like the world. Who get hyped during praise but sleep during conviction. We've exchanged repentance for relevance. But the truth is: if your Christianity never challenges your lifestyle, it's not Christianity—it's culture.

Hebrews 4:12 says the Word is *"living and active, sharper than any double-edged sword."* It should pierce. It should divide. It should reveal. When's the last time the Word broke you? When's the last time you left service wrestling with God instead of rating the worship?

The Responsibility Of The Pulpit

Pastors, leaders, shepherds—we bear responsibility. If our people can sit under us for years and never change, never feel convicted, never shift their behavior, we are not feeding them. We're entertaining them. We're babysitting spiritual infants who should be walking in power by now.

Ezekiel 33:7-9 speaks of the watchman. If he fails to warn the people, their blood is on his hands. It's time to preach truth again. To speak what God is saying, not what culture is selling. To restore the altar—not as a performance space, but as a place of transformation. Let the Spirit move again. Let the Word confront again. Let the sanctuary echo with repentance again.

Making Room For Conviction Again

Conviction is not cruelty, it's compassion. It's the voice of the Holy Spirit calling us back to alignment. It's proof that God hasn't given up on us.

Romans 2:4 says it is *"God's kindness that leads us to repentance."* When conviction disappears, so does the invitation to return.

We must welcome it again. In our preaching. In our worship. In our conversations. We must create sanctuaries where it's safe to repent. Where masks can fall. Where people can fall apart at the altar and find wholeness again. Let the silence be broken—not with noise, but with truth. Let the echo return—not of applause, but of knees hitting the floor.

Because where conviction is present, revival is possible. And without it, we're just playing church in a hollow room.

"GOD WILL INTERRUPT YOUR RITUAL JUST TO IGNITE YOUR FIRE AGAIN. DON'T LET ROUTINE EXTINGUISH THE REVIVAL MEANT TO LIVE IN YOU."

—Patricia S. Tanner

CHAPTER 14

THE POWER OF PERSONAL SURRENDER

• The Battle Of The Will-Surrender is not weakness.

• When Obedience Costs You-Your surrender should stretch your faith.

• Becoming a Living Sacrifice-A life of surrender is supernatural joy.

• Encouragement Over Everything-Encouragement is biblical.

• When Truth Offends-A time when truth is harsh and love sounds soft.

The righteous shall flourish like the palm tree: he shall grow like a cedar in Lebanon....

-Psalm 92:12

The Battle Of The Will

Surrender is not weakness—it's the greatest show of strength in the Kingdom. But it's also the hardest. We want control, predictability, and safety. But God asks for our will. Not just our habits, tithes, or attendance—but our deepest decisions. Surrender says, "Not my way, but Yours." It's a daily battle, but it's also the only path to victory.

Laying Down The Mask

Many of us have perfected spiritual performance. We know how to "do church." But personal surrender is private before it's ever public. It's what you do when no one is watching. Laying down the mask means admitting where you're still struggling, repenting where you're still compromising, and yielding where you're still resisting.

When Obedience Costs You

True surrender will cost you something—comfort, popularity, plans, sometimes people. Abraham had to leave his country. Esther had to risk her life. Jesus had to lay His down. If our obedience never stretches or scares us, we may not be surrendered. God isn't looking for half-hearted agreement; He's looking for full-hearted surrender.

Freedom Through Letting Go

The irony of surrender is that it leads to freedom. When you stop carrying what you weren't built to hold, peace floods in. When you let go of your idols, intimacy grows. When you release control, grace takes over. Surrender is not the end of your life—it's the beginning of the one God destined for you.

Becoming A Living Sacrifice

Romans 12:1 calls us to be *"living sacrifices."* That means ongoing surrender—not a one-time event, but a lifestyle. We climb off the altar when it gets hot, but God calls us back daily. A life of surrender is a life of supernatural joy, because it's aligned with divine purpose. The surrendered heart becomes the stage for God's greatest works.

The Gospel Of Good Vibes — When Encouragement Replaces Repentance

Cotton Candy Christianity

There's a version of the gospel being preached today that tastes sweet, feels good, and disappears quickly—leaving the soul starving. It's fluffy, comforting, and easy to digest.

But like cotton candy, it melts on contact and has no real nutritional value. It's what we now call "the gospel of good vibes." A message stripped of its urgency, depth, and demands, but full of positivity, empowerment, and self-affirmation.

This version of the gospel prioritizes feelings over faithfulness. It tells people they're enough but never tells them to repent. It celebrates purpose but avoids the cross. It affirms identity but denies sin. In trying to make the gospel more palatable, we've made it powerless. Because without repentance, there is no transformation.

Encouragement Over Everything

Encouragement is biblical. God is an encourager. His Word builds up and strengthens. But encouragement without correction becomes enablement. When people are constantly told "you're okay," even in their sin, we rob them of conviction. We soothe their wounds but never address the infection underneath.

2 Timothy 4:2 says, *"Preach the word; be prepared in season and out of season; correct, rebuke and encourage—with great patience and careful instruction."*

Notice the balance: correction and encouragement. Not one or the other. But today's churches often tip the scale toward motivation while avoiding confrontation.

Avoiding The Cross

The gospel is not just a feel-good message. It is a rescue mission. Jesus didn't die to give us comfort—He died to give us life. And that life requires surrender. **Luke 9:23** says, *"Whoever wants to be my disciple must deny themselves and take up their cross daily and follow me."*

But where is that call in modern preaching? Where is the invitation to die to self? Where is the teaching that suffering has a place in spiritual growth?

Instead, we tell people: *"You're destined for greatness," "God's going to open doors," "Your season is changing."* All of that may be true—but if there is no repentance, it is nothing more than spiritual flattery.

When Truth Offends

We now live in a time when truth sounds harsh and love sounds soft. People will leave a church because they were corrected. They'll unfollow a pastor for preaching about sin. They'll label biblical warnings as judgmental and call any form of discipline *"spiritual abuse."*

Galatians 4:16 poses Paul's question: *"Have I now become your enemy by telling you the truth?"* Real love tells the truth—even when it hurts. Real gospel preaching isn't afraid to wound if it leads to healing. Because without the diagnosis, there can be no cure.

The Gospel That Saves, Not Just Soothes

Jesus met people in their pain, yes. But He didn't leave them there. To the woman caught in adultery, He offered grace—but also told her, "Go and sin no more." To the rich man, He spoke of heaven—but also demanded surrender. To Nicodemus, He explained new birth—but also made it clear: "You must be born again."

We cannot skip the call to holiness. We cannot erase the cost of discipleship. The gospel saves us from sin, not just sadness. It invites us into transformation, not just tranquility.

Bringing Repentance Back

It's time to bring repentance back into our pulpits, our small groups, our conversations. Not as a weapon, but as a welcome. Not as condemnation, but as the first step to freedom. **Romans 2:4** says, *"It's God's kindness that leads us to repentance—not His anger."*

Encouragement is powerful when it comes after repentance. Grace is beautiful when it follows the truth. The most loving thing we can tell someone is that they need Jesus, they need forgiveness, and they need to change. Because that's where real healing begins.

The gospel is not just good vibes—it's good news. And good news only makes sense when we understand the bad news. We are sinners in need of a Savior. We are broken in need of a Healer. And we are loved, not because we're perfect, but because God is.

"THE TRUE CHURCH IS NOT STATIONARY—IT'S SENT. IT DOESN'T GATHER DUST IN BUILDINGS; IT MOVES IN POWER THROUGH SURRENDERED VESSELS."

—Patricia S. Tanner

CHAPTER 15

THE BENCH REJOICED

• The Day the Bench Emptied—What it looked like when people stood.

• From Waiting to Witnessing—The transformation of a congregation.

• Heaven Celebrates Movement—The joy of obedience and change.

• A New Generation of Movers—Youth rising into revival.

• And Still It Waits—For the next one to stand.

"Therefore, since we are surrounded by such a great cloud of witnesses, let us throw off everything that hinders… and let us run with perseverance the race marked out for us."
—Hebrews 12:1 (NIV)

The Silent Witness

Every bench in every church holds stories. Of those who came hoping. Of those who came hurting. Of those who never moved past hearing. The bench waits—not just physically, but spiritually. It represents every moment God invited, and someone postponed.

Every time truth was preached, and someone nodded but never knelt. It's not just a seat—it's a symbol of delay.

Missed Moments, Missed Mandates

What if the bench could talk? It would testify to missed callings, abandoned assignments, half-hearted worship, and unspoken cries. The tragedy isn't just those who never came to church—but those who came and never changed. God's Word went out, but it bounced off hardened hearts. The bench becomes a memorial of what could've been.

But God Still Waits

The beauty of God is that He waits longer than we deserve. He doesn't throw people away. The bench may symbolize delay, but grace turns delay into destiny. God still sends the Word. He still opens the door. He still calls your name, even if it's the hundredth time. The bench that waited can become the altar that launched.

From Benched To Burning

You don't have to end where you started. Your story can shift. The same bench that held your weight can now hold your witness. It can be the place you mark your "yes." The shift happens when you stand. When you walk to the altar. When you say, *"Here am I, send me."* You don't need another sermon; you need to surrender.

The Invitation Remains

This book is not just a reflection—it's an invitation. God is calling the benched believer back into the game. He is summoning the quiet hearts and the tired souls to rise again. There's still work to be done. There's still fire to carry. There are still people to reach. The bench that waited doesn't have to wait forever. The Kingdom is ready. Are you?

The Awakening — Returning To A Faith That Moves Us

The Sleepwalking Church

There is a growing grogginess that has settled over the modern church, spiritual sleep that looks like routine, sounds like religion, but lacks revelation. We worship out of memory instead of intimacy. We pray out of discipline instead of desperation. And we serve more out of habit than hunger.

Like someone walking through the motions in a dream, we are present but not fully awake. But God is sounding an alarm. The hour is urgent, and the slumber must end.

Romans 13:11 speaks directly to this generation: *"The hour has already come for you to wake up from your slumber, because our salvation is nearer now than when we first believed."*

This isn't just a call to awareness; it's a call to action. It's time for the Church to return to a faith that moves us—physically, emotionally, spiritually. A faith that doesn't just comfort but convicts. Faith that leads to fruit.

A Stirring In The Spirit

The awakening begins in the private place. Before it hits the pulpit, it must hit the heart. God is stirring individuals to get back to the basics—back to prayer, back to the Word, back to listening for His voice instead of just following trends. The awakening isn't a revival event with a flyer. It's an inner shift, a cry from deep calling unto deep.

You'll know the awakening has started when your tolerance for compromise decreases. When you no longer laugh at what grieves God. When your appetite for the presence becomes greater than your desire for applause. When you start asking again, "God, what do You want from me?"

Faith That Acts, Not Just Attends

James 2:17 says, *"Faith by itself, if it is not accompanied by action, is dead."* Yet, how many people sit on pews every Sunday, unmoved by truth, unchanged by grace? The awakening is not for spectators—it's for disciples. It doesn't just applaud sermons—it lives them. It doesn't just sing songs—it obeys the lyrics.

THE BENCH THAT WAITED

We must rediscover a faith that gets us out of our seats. That compels us to forgive, to serve, to give, to evangelize, to heal, to disciple. A faith that costs us something. That burns bridges with sin. That breaks generational cycles. That refuses to play church and insists on being the Church.

Returning To The Fire

There is a fire that burns in the awakened heart. It is not emotional hype. It is not circumstantial excitement. It is the holy flame of the Spirit that purifies and propels.

Jeremiah said in **20:9,** *"His word is in my heart like a fire, a fire shut up in my bones. I am weary of holding it in."*

We must ask God to reignite this fire. We must fan the flame through repentance and intimacy. We must separate from what dulls the spark—distractions, sin, spiritual laziness. The awakening cannot happen where we are cozy with compromise. It only erupts in surrendered hearts.

A Church That Cannot Be Ignored

The final result of the awakening is a Church that is impossible to ignore. Not because of its size, but because of its light. Not because of its aesthetics, but because of its anointing. When the Church wakes up, demons tremble.

Communities change.

Families are restored.

Cities are impacted.

Acts 17:6 describes the early believers as *"those who have turned the world upside down."* That is what awakened faith looks like— bold, alive, and disruptive to darkness. We are not called to blend in. We are called to burn. And the world will only feel the heat if we stop pressing snooze on the Spirit.

It's time. Time to rise. Time to repent. Time to return.

The bench is no longer your seat, it's your launchpad.

Wake up, Church. Your movement starts now.

"WHEN OBEDIENCE STANDS UP, EVEN THE BENCH GIVES PRAISE. HEAVEN REJOICES WHEN MOVEMENT BEGINS."

—Patricia S. Tanner

CONCLUSION

Get Off The Bench:
The Call To Live, Move, And Multiply The Truth

This book began with a simple image: a bench, sitting in the back of the sanctuary, waiting for its occupants to rise. But the bench is more than a piece of wood or a resting place in a church. It symbolizes missed moments, paused purposes, and potential left untouched. It's where so many sit—physically present but spiritually parked—showing up week after week but never stepping fully into who God created them to be.

The message woven through these pages is not one of condemnation, but of confrontation. We must confront the ways we've settled for less. Confront the comfortable routines that have replaced radical obedience. Confront the way we've traded fire for form, conviction for compliments, and truth for trends. The Spirit of God is calling us to awaken from passivity, to stir up the gifts within us, and to walk boldly into the identity and purpose we've been given.

This is not about performing religion, it's about living kingdom. It's not about looking holy but becoming whole. We were never called to just attend church—we were called to *be* the Church. And that requires action. It requires risk. It requires a willingness to stand when others sit, to speak when silence is safer, to move when everything in you wants to stay still.

If you've felt disconnected, numb, or like you've been stuck on pause—this is your moment. You don't have to have all the answers. You don't have to be perfect. But you do have to rise.

Because the world is aching for truth. Your family is watching. Your coworkers are curious. Your community is starving for authenticity. And heaven is waiting for your yes.

Don't just read this book. Let it read you. Let it dig into the hidden places where you've settled and stir a new urgency. Let it call you out of shallow waters into the deep end of faith. Let it remind you that you are not too broken, not too late, and not too far gone.

Now is the time. Not tomorrow. Not when you feel ready. Now. Get off the bench of religion and step into the movement of purpose. Let your life be a sermon. Let your obedience be your offering. Let your surrender be your starting line.

And when you've risen—when you've stepped out—don't stop there.

Help someone else stand. Speak life into those still slumped in shame. Encourage the weary. Correct with love. Serve with humility. And most of all, multiply what you've learned. The world doesn't just need preachers—it needs doers. It needs witnesses. It needs people who have climbed off the bench and into the battlefield.

So, take a breath. Say a prayer. And take that first step. Your seat has been empty long enough.

The Kingdom needs your movement. Get up.

And don't look back.

PATRICIA S. TANNER

ABOUT THE AUTHOR

Patricia Tanner was born and raised in Sanford FL. She comes from a family of three siblings. Patricia Tanner is the founder of Multhai International Realty, Multhai Asset Management Services, and Multhai Investment Group which is located in Sanford, Florida. She is a graduate of the University of Central Florida, where she received a Bachelor of Science in Business Administration and a minor in Human Resources Management.

Patricia began her career shortly thereafter as a Regional Property Manager in the apartment community. Throughout her career in property management, she has built interpersonal relationships with corporate clients. She has a successful track record of increasing company revenues over $5 million annually, through hard work, commitment, creativeness, and strategic planning.

Her experience and leadership role eventually led her to achieve a Florida Real Estate Broker license. She spent fifteen years in the Real Estate field while completing a Master of Arts in Human Resources Management from Webster University, and a Master of Public Administration from Troy University. It was in this capacity that she decided to open her own brokerage company, Multhai International Realty.

In addition, Patricia finds time in her busy to participate in her own Non For Profit Organization, Stones 2 Homes. She remains President of her organization in which she helps people build, keep, or purchase homes in affordable communities. She is the founder of PNT Property Partners in which she buys vacant land, develops them, and constructs brand new construction homes in Sanford Florida. Her overall goal is to educate and provide resources to help people overcome financial hardships and credit disadvantage to live the American Dream through homeownership in spite of economic hardship. Through her visions she will continue to grow as an entrepreneur and is willing to share her knowledge, experience, and expertise with anyone whom is willing to learn.

MORE BOOKS BY THE AUTHOR

30 Days Of Grieving
Given By The Inspiration Of God
Healing From COVID-19

Almost a year later, and it hit me... My mother was gone, and I was still stuck at the hospital. I had tried everything from crying to counseling, and even prayer. Pray they told me. Trust God they insisted. But it seemed as if nothing was working. I was hurt, dealing with my reality: my mother was not coming back.

While journeying through grief, it was under the divine 'Inspiration of God' that He placed me in a trance. While I was gaining a revelation about grief, He gave me this journal, '30 Days Of Grieving.'

NOW AVAILABLE:
WWW.Amazon.Com

PATRICIA S. TANNER

The 30 Days Challenge:

I Tested POSITIVE for COVID-19

If you had 30 days to live, what would you do? If you were told that you needed to prepare for a marathon in 30 days and you were completely out of shape, what would you do first? If a family member handed you one million dollars and told you that you had to figure out how to build a house (debt free), how would you execute your plan?

I'm catching you off guard with these requests, right? Well, this is exactly what COVID-19 did when it snatched my mother's life away, wrecking my entire world. I had to battle for my mother AND my faith in 30 days flat. What a challenge!

Throughout this book, I will walk you through my brief journey with COVID-19, negative of a happy ending. I will share the diary I kept while attending to my mother, and the scriptures I read, prayed, and quoted as my shield and protection.

Take the journey with me, there is healing on the other side!

NOW AVAILABLE:
WWW.Amazon.Com

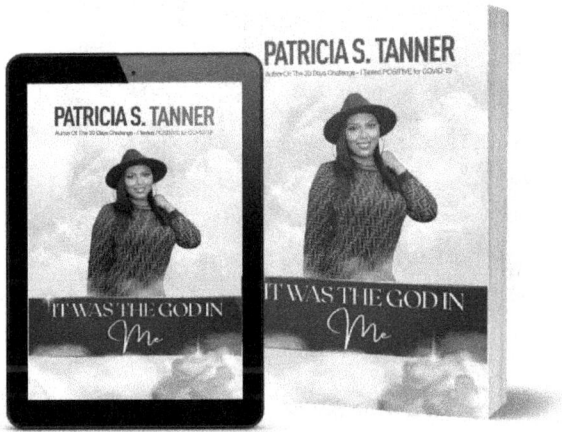

It Was The God In

Me

Success can be attributed to many things. Depending on the person who has obtained success would determine those to whom they attribute their success. Some give credit to their daily routine while others give credit to a mentor or some sort of system they followed. When I think about my success, the only person who I can give the credit to is God.

In this memoir, I share the successes and failures I have experienced throughout my life. From my individual experiences to my entrepreneurial journey, I share how God has walked with me every step of the way.

Come and see.. It Was The God In Me!!

NOW AVAILABLE:
WWW.Amazon.Com

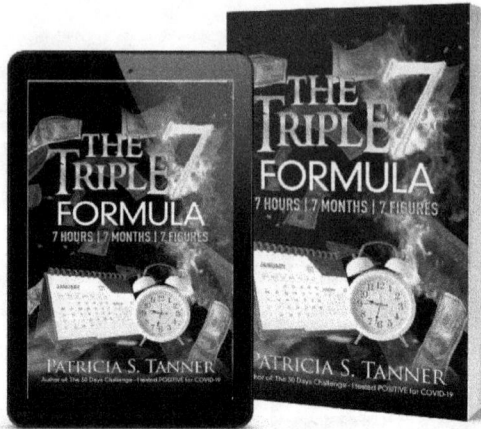

The Triple 7 Formula is designed for business owners who are looking forward to hitting the million-dollar mark in their business. If you own a business and seem to be running in financial circles, this book will get you on track to simultaneously gaining sound business structure and millions in your bank account.

It was through many conversations with business owners in lack of financial gain that prompted Patricia to share her blueprint for millionaire status. Through this book, she demonstrates how to gain financial ground by developing strong teams, implementing systems, and setting stackable goals. If you are ready to gain a laser sharp focus, and implement these clear steps, you will position yourself for financial greatness. Your business will be sound, and you will see financial growth beyond your wildest dreams!!

NOW AVAILABLE:
WWW.Amazon.Com

THE BENCH THAT WAITED

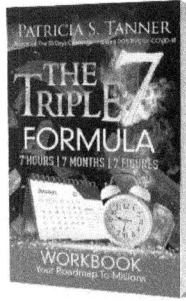

The Triple 7 Formula is specifically crafted for business owners aspiring to reach the million-dollar milestone. If you are a business owner feeling stuck in financial cycles, this book will set you on the path to building both a solid business structure and financial success.

This workbook is designed to complement the textbook of the same name. As you progress through its pages, you will be inspired to take decisive steps toward becoming a millionaire. From constructing your business framework to creating the millionaire's avatar, this process will expand your knowledge and mindset. Not only will you chart a course to financial success, but you will also identify your accountability circle and select a mentor to guide you toward greatness.

I cannot guarantee millionaire status unless you actively follow the steps to begin your journey. If you are searching for a get rich quick scheme, this workbook is not for you. I am looking for those ready to put in the effort—and since you are reading this, I believe that's you!

You have finally found it: Your roadmap to millions!

NOW AVAILABLE:
WWW.Amazon.Com

PATRICIA S. TANNER

Can Salvation Get You Into Heaven? The Answer Is Yes! offers a powerful and biblically grounded exploration of God's eternal plan, revealing the heart of the Gospel and the assurance of salvation through Jesus Christ. Unpacking life's most vital questions—Who is God? Why were we created? What does Jesus' life mean for us?—this book brings clarity to the believer's journey and confirms that salvation, once received, is eternally secure. Whether you're seeking understanding or affirming your faith, this inspiring guide will lead you into the confidence and joy of knowing heaven is your eternal home.

NOW AVAILABLE:
WWW.Amazon.Com

Find Patricia on The Web:

www.PatriciaTanner.com

Follow Patricia on social media:

Facebook & Instagram: @PatriciaTannerInc

PATRICIA S. TANNER